DAILY LIFE IN US HISTORY

# LIFE DURING THE INDUSTRIAL REVOLUTION

by Julia Garstecki

Content Consultant
Jamie Bronstein
Professor of History
New Mexico State University

Core Library

An Imprint of Abdo Publishing
www.abdopublishing.com

www.abdopublishing.com

Published by Abdo Publishing, a division of ABDO, PO Box 398166,
Minneapolis, Minnesota 55439. Copyright © 2015 by Abdo Consulting
Group, Inc. International copyrights reserved in all countries. No part of
this book may be reproduced in any form without written permission from
the publisher. Core Library™ is a trademark and logo of Abdo Publishing.

Printed in the United States of America, North Mankato, Minnesota
092014
012015

Cover Photo: North Wind Picture Archives/AP Images
Interior Photos: North Wind Picture Archives, 4, 6, 8, 10, 12, 15, 27, 32,
38, 42, 45; Detroit Publishing Co./Library of Congress, 17; AP Images, 18;
Red Line Editorial, 21, 30; Lewis Wickes Hine/Library of Congress, 24, 28;
Library of Congress, 35

Editor: Ethan Hiedeman
Series Designer: Becky Daum

Library of Congress Control Number: 2014944211

Cataloging-in-Publication Data
Garstecki, Julia.
 Life during the Industrial Revolution / Julia Garstecki.
   p. cm. -- (Daily life in US history)
 ISBN 978-1-62403-627-9 (lib. bdg.)
 Includes bibliographical references and index.
 1. Industrial Revolution--United States--Social aspects--Juvenile literature.
 2. Industries--United States--History--Juvenile literature.  3. United States--
 Economic conditions--To 1865--Juvenile literature.   I. Title.
 330.973--dc23
                                                    2014944211

# CONTENTS

# CHAPTER ONE

# FROM FARMS TO FACTORIES

T he thought of moving your body from this crowded bed is more than you can handle. Your roommates are getting dressed. They whisper that you will get in trouble if you miss the next bell. A girl, not much older than your 14 years, hands you a wad of cotton to put in your ears.

"Here," she tells you. "It will dull the sound. You won't get a headache if you wear them."

Many children in the Industrial Revolution found work in factories.

New inventions such as the Bessemer steel converter spurred economic change.

Every part of your body screams with pain as you sit up. But your family needs every penny it can get. This factory pays more than the others, and you are grateful for the work.

## The Rise of Industry

Can you imagine working in a factory 12 hours a day? During the period in US history known as the Industrial Revolution, many children began doing just that. When people think of a revolution, they usually think of bloody soldiers and smoky battlefields.

However, the Industrial Revolution didn't involve any battle plans. The Industrial Revolution was the transition from an agricultural economy to one based on manufacturing. The Industrial Revolution began in Great Britain in the late 1700s. During this time, many British citizens immigrated to the United States. They brought their knowledge and experience of the technological innovations in Britain. Soon the United States was experiencing its own Industrial

## PERSPECTIVES

# Native Americans and the Industrial Revolution

European settlement in North America devastated Native American populations. Millions of Native Americans lost their lives to disease and warfare. More Native Americans were forced off lands they had lived on for thousands of years as European colonists expanded west. The newcomers hunted bison, which many Native Americans depended on for survival, nearly to extinction. The US government forced Native Americans off western land so white settlers could use the land to grow crops. For Native Americans, the Industrial Revolution caused even more of their customs to be lost.

Cyrus McCormick's reaper revolutionized agriculture and allowed food to be grown more cheaply.

Revolution. All aspects of life in the United States transformed starting around 1820. New technology during this time created a demand for even more mass production and industry. The transformation continued until approximately the start of World War I (1914–1918).

Before the Industrial Revolution, economics in the United States had not changed much for hundreds of years. Most Americans grew their own food and made their own tools and clothes. During the Industrial Revolution, technology improved at a rapid rate.

Machines took over much of the work people had done before. People across the United States went from working in the fields to working in factories. They earned a wage instead of growing and selling food. They bought what they needed in stores instead of making it themselves or trading for it. In just one century, manufacturing, communication, and transportation changed around the world.

## Sparks of Revolution

Inventors set off the sparks of the Industrial Revolution by imagining new methods of doing work. The first textile factory in the

## The World's Fair

The first World's Fair took place in London, England, in 1851. It was a chance for the countries of the world to show off their new machines and inventions to the rest of the world. It was organized by Great Britain's Prince Albert, who wanted to showcase Great Britain to an international audience. The exhibits included technological advances from all over the world. More than 6 million people visited the exhibition, ensuring it would become a tradition for years to come.

Textile mills used spinning mules, big machines that spun cotton and other fabrics.

United States was created in 1790. These factories created cotton for clothes. Some machines, such as the telegraph, made communication easier. Improvements in transportation, such as the railroad, meant that products could reach people outside the city much more quickly and easily.

Growing populations, especially in cities, created demand for the new products. There were more consumers than ever before. Workers were needed to produce the products.

By the 1850s, machines and factories were everywhere. Better clothing, kitchenware, and tools were now widely available. The United States had transformed from an agricultural-based economy to an industrial economy. Two out of three people now worked in manufacturing or service jobs.

## EXPLORE ONLINE

Chapter One focuses on the beginning of the Industrial Revolution and some of its causes. The website below gives another take on the beginning of the Industrial Revolution in the United States. As you know, every source is different. How is the information given in the website different from the information in this chapter? What information is the same? How do the two sources present information differently? What can you learn from this website?

**History Times: The Industrial Revolution**
www.mycorelibrary.com/industrial-revolution

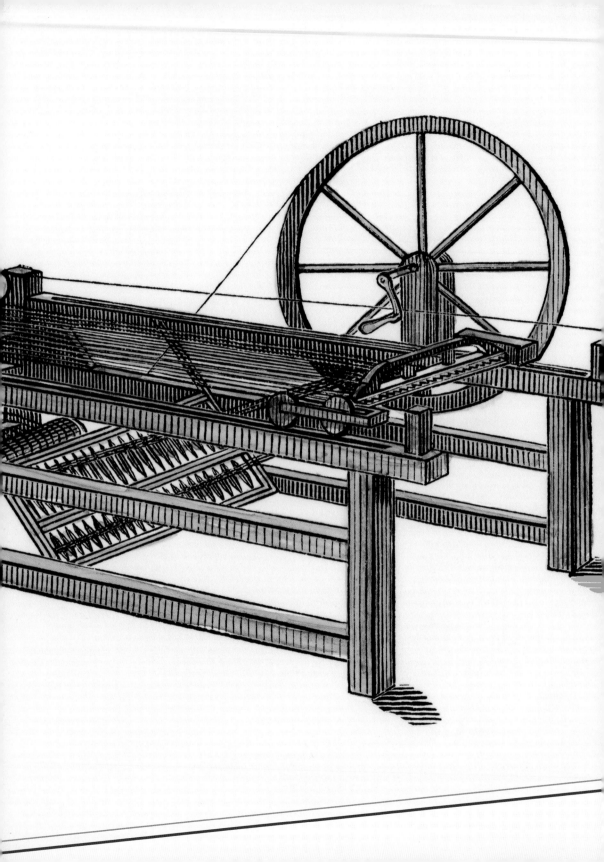

# CHAPTER TWO

# WORK DURING THE INDUSTRIAL REVOLUTION

The machines invented during the Industrial Revolution changed the way work was done. Improvements in technology changed the sorts of jobs workers did, and in some cases put them out of work.

Textile mills were extremely important in the Industrial Revolution. Until the 1700s, workers called spinners made yarn out of wool, cotton, or flax,

The spinning jenny helped industrialize the textile industry.

using simple tools such as the spinning wheel. British inventor James Hargreaves patented the spinning jenny in 1770. This machine allowed one person to spin eight strings at a time.

Mass-produced clothes were much cheaper than handmade ones. More people began buying their clothes rather than making them themselves. Before the Industrial Revolution, the creation of textiles was a cottage industry. A cottage industry takes place in people's homes. But with the creation of machines such as the spinning jenny, textile workers began to work in factories instead of their homes. They left home every morning to work in the factory rather than producing smaller quantities of yarn and fabric that they would sell themselves.

## The Cotton Economy

The new speed of spinning led to greater demand for cotton. The cotton gin, developed by Eli Whitney in 1793, quickly separated cotton seeds from usable fibers. Before, this work had been done mostly by

The cotton gin increased production of cotton, which led to Southern planters using more slaves in their fields.

black slaves using only their hands. The cotton gin meant that slaves could produce more clean cotton faster. The cotton gin allowed the American South to produce much more cotton. The South became one of the wealthiest regions in the world. Unfortunately, one

## Slaves

In 1860 there were 4 million slaves living in the South. Most worked on cotton and tobacco farms. Slaves started work at sunrise. They continued to work as long as the moon provided enough light. The cotton that each slave had picked during the day was weighed each night to ensure the slave had worked hard. If slaves' loads were too light, their master might beat them. For dinner, slaves would get another meal, often of cold bacon and corn. Many slept in windowless cabins made of logs. Many lived near animals in areas contaminated by animal feces. Slaves could not own any property of their own. Half of children born to slaves died before they turned one.

side effect of the booming cotton industry was the increase of slavery. Now that cotton was so much more profitable, more slaves were forced to work harvesting cotton. Slaves were not paid for their work. They were often beaten and underfed. Since slaves were bought and sold as property, they were often separated from their families.

Plantation owners kept the profits earned from their cotton, making them very rich.

The *Clermont* had two paddle wheels with diameters of 15 feet (4.6 m).

By 1815, the South was producing 93 million pounds (42 million kg) of cotton each year.

## A Transportation Revolution

Before the Industrial Revolution, people used simple wooden vessels called flatboats to transport goods or passengers on rivers. Flatboats were slow-moving and awkward to navigate. In the late 1700s, mechanics and scientists began to develop boats powered by steam engines that could carry large amounts of cargo as well as passengers. The ships carried passengers

The Erie Canal, which connected New York City and the Great Lakes when it was finished in 1825, spurred canal building across the United States.

and freight up and down the Mississippi and other major US waterways.

The Mississippi and Hudson rivers soon became water highways with many kinds of steamboats. Some carried goods such as flour, cotton, coal, or mail. Others carried people. People could make trips in weeks that would have taken months before. These steamboats created jobs in river towns for the boats' crew members. Trade of goods up and down the river also made communities along the rivers wealthier. People were needed to build, maintain, and drive the boats. Steamboats remained popular until locomotives became faster and could travel farther than rivers and canals allowed.

The earliest steamboats were cramped and uncomfortable for both crew and passengers. But as steam engines improved and got bigger and more powerful, the ships grew with them.

By the mid-1800s, some large steamboats were as stylish as the fanciest hotels. Wealthy passengers enjoyed traveling up- and downriver in rooms decorated with fine paintings, rugs, and furniture. The steamboats also featured the finest food, music, and other entertainment. The luxurious ships were much more comfortable than most kinds of sea travel people of that time were familiar with.

## By Rail

In the early 1800s, engineers in Great Britain and the United States created steam-powered rail cars called locomotives. Before the use of the steam engine, train cars had moved along rails by human or horse power.

The steam locomotive made it possible to move heavy loads long distances by rail.

By 1850 railroads were common. The railroad industry offered thousands of jobs that included building and maintaining the locomotives, laying track, and operating the trains. Chinese immigrants laid much of the track in the West. They could lay miles of track a day and used explosives to cut through mountains. Hundreds were killed in accidents with explosives, in avalanches, and by the harsh weather. Pay could also be very low for immigrant workers. Sometimes they did not have enough food.

As tracks were laid throughout the country, cities connected by them such as Buffalo, New York, Chicago, Illinois, and Saint Louis, Missouri, grew. People and goods could now travel quickly and easily from town to town. In 1869 the first transcontinental freight train left California and arrived in New York a week later. Americans now had greater access to goods regardless of where they lived and could travel

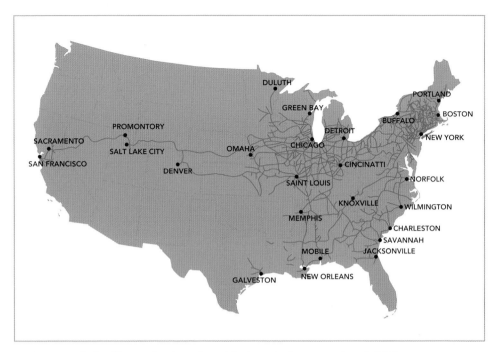

Map of Railroads in the United States in 1870
The map shows how railroads spread through the United States in the mid-1800s. After reading about the introduction of railroads into the country, why do you think they were built where they were? How do you think the railroads connected different parts of the country?

farther and faster. Before the railroad it could take half a year to cross the country. Now you could do it in five days for less than $200.

## The Telegraph

Advances in communication also brought people closer together. Samuel F. B. Morse, a teacher of art and design, invented the telegraph in 1837.

## Patents

A patent gives an inventor ownership of his or her creation. After receiving a patent, the inventor has control over his or her product and can decide how it will be used. This way, the inventor gets paid for the invention. During the Industrial Revolution, many inventors worked on steamboats and railroads. This created arguments about who would get the patent and the money from various inventions. Legal action was often the only way to settle such disputes. A judge would decide who would get credit for the invention. Whoever the judge chose could become a very wealthy person.

The telegraph used wires to send messages immediately across long distances. The messages came in the form of dots and dashes that represented letters. This language became known as Morse Code. Soon telegraph wires connected cities and towns across the country. Americans could now communicate with each other faster than ever before. Those living in the West no longer had to wait weeks or months to find out what was happening in the East.

Factory workers wrote songs to raise awareness of their poor working conditions:

> Strike, strike, the Workers anvil,
>
> For the cause of Labor,
>
> Strike for your home and freedom,
>
> For each friend and neighbor.
>
> Every one For this great cause And Reform laws,
>
> Now demand complete protection.
>
> Strike, strike, the fire is glowing—
>
> Heed ye not the minions,
>
> Seeking to capture Labor, And to clip the pinions
>
> Of our clan. Will you grant all At the first call,
>
> And submit to party factions

Source: "Music for the Nation: American Sheet Music." American Memory. Library of Congress. Web. Accessed August 26, 2014.

## Consider Your Audience

Review this passage closely. Consider how you would adapt this song for a different audience, such as your parents, your principal, or younger friends. Write a blog post conveying this same information for the new audience. How does your new approach differ from the original text and why?

# CHAPTER THREE

# CHILDREN AT WORK AND AT SCHOOL

As factories grew, owners needed more workers. They looked to children. Children could be paid less than adults. Their small size also let them do certain jobs that were too delicate for adults. At the time, there were no successful federal laws that banned child labor in the United States.

Children as young as five worked in the seafood industry, shucking oysters and peeling shrimp.

## Immigrant Workers

Immigrants from Germany, Ireland, and England poured into the United States during the Industrial Revolution. They sought a better life. Most thought the United States would provide greater opportunities than their home countries. But employers did not treat their immigrant workers fairly. Employers often paid immigrants lower wages than other workers. Immigrants also faced discrimination and were treated poorly by Americans. Many settled in communities made up of others from their homelands. The immigrants of the Industrial Revolution helped make the United States the diverse nation it is today.

# Girls in the Workforce

The most common industrial employment for girls between ages seven and fourteen was the textile mill. Girls could earn between 80 cents and $1.40 per week. The money helped their families buy food and other necessities.

Girls often lived in a boardinghouse, where a matron was in charge. Five or six girls shared a bedroom. Two or three girls might share one bed, and many girls shared one bathroom. Workdays were

Girls in textile mills worked with the windows closed even in summer to provide ideal conditions for making thread.

12 hours long, six days a week. Many different jobs were available, depending on the size of the girl.

Young girls were more common than young boys in the textile mills. Their small size made it easy for them to change spinners or bobbins, which were used to gather new thread. They replaced spindles and tied broken threads. Children could slip in between machines to fix small parts with their small fingers. The jobs were dangerous. Most machines lacked safety features to prevent fingers from getting caught in their mechanisms. Breathing in lint from the cotton all day could cause a fatal disease called brown lung.

Breaker boys breathed in coal dust on their long shifts, which harmed their lungs.

## Boys in the Workforce

While girls were more likely to find work in textile mills, many boys found other jobs that were just as difficult. In Pennsylvania and Virginia, boys commonly worked in coal mines. The mines provided coal for steamboats, railroads, and factories.

Boys working in coal mines did a number of tasks. Boys as young as seven worked as "breaker boys." They crouched while breaking coal from rock for up to 12 hours a day. Older boys took care of the mules that hauled the coal. Others operated ventilation doors that kept toxic gases from building up in the mines. Explosions, poisonous gas leaks, and other accidents were common. Lead and dust from coal and rock were also dangerous.

Many children from poor families worked up to 90 hours a week to help support their families.

## Education Reform

Some adults believed all children should have the right to attend school and should not have to work. Many people believed children should not work in factories. One of the first public schools opened in Saint Louis, Missouri, in 1808. Many one-room schoolhouses followed. Students of all ages traveled by foot or in horse-drawn buggies to learn in one of the new schoolhouses. The youngest students

### about 1765
### steam engine

James Watt's improved steam engine paved the way for the steamboat and locomotive.

### about 1770
### spinning jenny

The speedy spinning of wool and other fabrics led to the industrialization of the textile industry.

### about 1793
### cotton gin

By speeding up the cotton cleaning process, Eli Whitney's cotton gin inadvertently led to the use of more slaves.

### about 1807
### steamboat

Robert Fulton's steamboat begins regular service.

### about 1836
### telegraph

Samuel Morse's invention allows information to be transported more quickly than ever.

### about 1844
### sewing machine

Elias Howe's machine allowed clothes to be made quickly and cheaply in factories.

**Timeline of Major Inventions during the Industrial Revolution**

This timeline shows some of the major inventions that spurred change during the Industrial Revolution. What does seeing the inventions in chronological order tell you about how they may have developed? Why might later inventions have needed earlier ones to be invented first?

received their lessons in the morning before they became too tired. Students also helped care for their schoolhouse. They carried firewood to keep it warm in winter, cleaned it as needed, and helped repair the structure as it aged.

After their long hours in the mill, some girls read magazines and books kept in the boardinghouses. A group of inspired women created *The Lowell Offering*, a 16-page magazine with original works written by the factory girls in Lowell. A factory girl wrote about the hardships of life in an excerpt from the article "The Spirit of Discontent" in an 1841 *Offering*:

> *I am going home, where I shall not be obliged to rise so early in the morning, nor be dragged about by the factory bell, nor confined in a close noisy room from morning to night. I shall not stay here. . . . Up before day, at the clang of the bell, and out of the mill by the clang of the bell—into the mill, and at work in obedience to that ding-dong of a bell—just as though we were so many living machines.*
>
> Source: Almira. "The Spirit of Discontent." The Lowell Offering July, 1841: 111–114.
> Print. 111.

## What's the Big Idea?

Take a close look at this excerpt. What is the writer's main point about life in a factory? Pick out two details she uses to make this point. What can you tell about the quality of life for factory workers based on this excerpt?

# CHAPTER FOUR

# FROM COUNTRY TO CITY

The Industrial Revolution changed how people lived. Now men and women could take wage-earning jobs in the growing factories.

Women were still the primary caregivers for their children. Though they no longer needed to make as much clothing for their families, they did the washing and mending. Women still cooked and cleaned the home. Many women helped support their families

Women were in demand as workers in textile factories.

## The Labor Movement

Factory owners could make more money if they paid their workers low wages and did not invest in safety measures. To protect themselves, workers began uniting to form organized groups called unions that fought for better wages and safer living conditions. The formation of such unions was called the labor movement. Unions protested together to let factory owners know they were being unfair. Unions would also go on strike, which meant their members refused to work until factory owners met their demands.

by working in factories. These women often relied on older family members, neighbors, or even older children to care for the younger ones while they were at work.

## The Growth of Cities

Before factory jobs drew them to the cities, many more people lived in the country and farmed. One major city, Chicago, had 300,000 inhabitants in 1870. By 1890 there were more than 1 million. Most warehouses, factories, and docks were in the center of the cities. By the late 1800s, streetcars, railroads, and

Cities such as Chicago boomed in the late 1800s and early 1900s as workers moved in to take up new industrial jobs.

trolleys enabled cities to expand because people did not have to live within walking distance of their jobs.

Most people chose to live near those who shared their culture and financial status. Immigrants sought out others from their home countries to live with. They ate food and spoke languages that reminded them of home.

## Mental Illness

During the Industrial Revolution the mentally ill often lived in awful conditions. Sometimes boys, girls, and adults with mental disabilities were placed in prisons with violent criminals. Others were sent to hospitals known as asylums. The mentally ill were put into cribs or strapped to beds or chairs. Most of these people lacked heat and access to a bathroom. Sometimes they were beaten. In 1841 a reformer named Dorothea Dix witnessed the awful conditions in the hospitals. She convinced local and federal governments to build new hospitals and change how they were run.

The working poor, those who were employed but still fell below the poverty line, included many new immigrants. These workers filled the cities and worked many of the new jobs created by the Industrial Revolution. They lived in small apartments near the factories in which they worked. Landlords made money by renting to the many families that moved to the city for jobs.

Government services could not keep up with the quick growth of the cities. Clean water, garbage collection, and sewage systems were not sufficient, contributing to poor living conditions. The biggest problem with the cramped living spaces and poor sanitation systems was the outbreak of illnesses, such as cholera, in the cities. This caused illness and even death throughout the late 1800s.

## FURTHER EVIDENCE

This chapter discusses the changing roles of men and women during the Industrial Revolution. What is the main point of this chapter? What key evidence supports this point? Go to the article on the Industrial Revolution at the website below. Find a quote from the website that supports the chapter's main point. Does the quote support an existing piece of evidence in the chapter? Or does it add a new one?

### Women and the Early Industrial Revolution in the United States

www.mycorelibrary.com/industrial-revolution

# CHAPTER FIVE

# IMPACTS

The Industrial Revolution brought many positive changes to the United States. Goods became cheaper. Technological advances helped doctors save more lives. But the Industrial Revolution had many problems. Pollution was a big issue. Coal was necessary for transportation, but the negative side effects included soot and smog. Breathing coal waste could cause serious health problems.

Smog and soot were dangerous by-products of many factories during the Industrial Revolution.

## Medical Advances

The Industrial Revolution brought greater understanding of how diseases spread. Doctors learned that washing their hands before surgery kept patients from dying. Others discovered that polluted water spread disease. New rules and advances in sewage technology helped prevent the spread of disease.

## An Industrial Nation

The United States completely transformed

from a nation of farmers to one of factories in less than a century. Manufacturing, transportation, and communication technology were all transformed during the Industrial Revolution. The inventions of the early and mid-1800s created a need for more production as the quality of life improved for Americans. The cities swelled as the countryside emptied. For most Americans, life had changed forever.

## Industry and the Civil War

The Civil War was fought between the Northern and Southern states within America from 1861 to 1865, during the Industrial Revolution. Most of the factories and industries were located in the North. Soldiers in the North could travel to battle by train. Machines used in farming helped families in the North keep up with production while the men were away in battle. Factories actually grew and improved to produce weapons, uniforms, and tools for the war effort. The North's advantage in factories and industries helped it win the Civil War.

# A DAY IN THE LIFE

Thomas is a 12-year-old boy working in a mill. The money Thomas makes at the mill helps his family buy the food and clothes they need for his younger siblings.

**4:30 a.m.**
Thomas's father wakes him up. Thomas washes and gets dressed for a long day of work.

**5:00 a.m.**
Thomas scarfs down oatcakes and gruel, a thin soup made from oats, potatoes, milk, and water. It is not very tasty, but it fills him up for the long day ahead.

**5:30 a.m.**
Thomas runs to the mill. It is raining, but the mill operates in all kinds of weather.

**6:00 a.m.**
Thomas starts work. The big machine called the mule starts up. It spins fiber into cloth. Thomas stands by with an oil can. He oils the tops and bottoms of the spindles to keep the mule running.

## 12:00 p.m.

Thomas gets a half-hour break for lunch. He eats bread and mutton. He drinks dirty water. The machines run even while the workers eat.

## 2:00 p.m.

Thomas repairs one of the mule's straps that broke. It is skilled work, not something you could just come in off the street and do without training.

## 3:00 p.m.

Thomas keeps equipment clean throughout the day even as he attends to other duties. He sweeps the floor and cleans machine parts.

## 8:00 p.m.

The bell rings. Thomas's day at work is finally over. Exhausted, he makes the trek back home. It is no longer raining. Thomas can smell the stench of the stockyards nearby and hear the clatter of the locomotives that roll in and out.

## 8:15 p.m.

Thomas arrives home. He eats dinner with his family— vegetable soup and milk.

## 9:00 p.m.

Thomas goes to sleep. He has another long day of work at the mill tomorrow.

## Why Do I Care?

The Industrial Revolution paved the way for the standard of living most Americans have enjoyed since. Manufacturing, transportation, and communication were greatly improved during this era. How do the inventions of the Industrial Revolution impact your life now?

## Take a Stand

In Chapter Two you read that patent owners can decide how their inventions can be used. Do you think it's fair for a patent owner to be able to stop others from using and improving on his or her idea? Why or why not? Write a paragraph defending your position. Use evidence from the text to support your view.

## You Are There

Imagine you are about to take your first ride on a new machine—the locomotive! How would it feel to travel out West for the first time? Imagine what you see and hear as you travel farther from home than ever before. Investigate the map in Chapter Two. Where would you want to go?

## Say What?

You learned a lot of new things about machines in this book. Pick five new machine-related words that you learned. Use a dictionary to help you understand what the words mean. Teach a friend about these new words.

# GLOSSARY

**consumer**
a person who purchases goods and services for personal use

**flax**
a blue-flowered plant that can be used for textile fiber

**industrial economy**
an economy based on factories and the mass production of goods instead of on agriculture

**mass production**
the creation of large amounts of the same product, usually made on assembly lines

**matron**
a woman in charge of domestic and medical arrangements at a boarding school or establishment

**products**
articles or substances that are manufactured for sale

**textile**
a type of cloth or woven fabric

**trading**
the action of buying and selling goods and services

# LEARN MORE

## Books

Grayson, Robert. *The US Industrial Revolution.* Edina, MN: ABDO, 2011.

Mullenbach, Cheryl. *The Industrial Revolution for Kids: The People and Technology That Changed the World, with 21 Activities.* Chicago: Chicago Review Press, 2014.

Van Zee, Amy. *The Rise of Industry: 1870–1900.* Edina, MN: ABDO, 2014.

## Websites

To learn more about Daily Life in US History, visit **booklinks.abdopublishing.com**. These links are routinely monitored and updated to provide the most current information available.

Visit **www.mycorelibrary.com** for free additional tools for teachers and students.

# INDEX

# ABOUT THE AUTHOR

Julia Garstecki is a writer and teacher who lives in western New York. She attended Michigan State University, State University of New York Fredonia, and Buffalo State University. She loves researching and writing about new things!